# Luv is

## Quotes from children

### Jessica Zavala

This book is dedicated to Jordon Benson who taught me the meaning of endless love for another. That love is constant and utterly unconditional

Balboa Press books may be ordered through booksellers or by contacting:

Balboa Press
A Division of Hay House
1663 Liberty Drive
Bloomington, IN 47403
www.balboapress.com
1 (877) 407-4847

ISBN: 978-1-5043-7600-6 (sc)
ISBN: 978-1-5043-7601-3 (e)

Library of Congress Control Number: 2017909275

Print information available on the last page.

Balboa Press rev. date: 05/25/2018

BALBOA.
PRESS
A DIVISION OF HAY HOUSE

# Contents

This book is dedicated to my beautiful daughter Jolene whom inspired all of this. You have made me so proud and you amaze me every day. I can hardly wait to see what you'll do next. You keep the wind blowing through my sails... Mommy loves you!

And to Jordon Benson, the love of my life. He has taught me that love surely knows no end. It endures relentlessly and effortlessly. I'll always love you, no matter what. Hill or high water. In the midst of a storm. To the moon and back. Even if our paths lead us forever astray.

Love… There are many ways to interpret the word, to each of us it takes on its own form. It also changes as we get older and as we encounter new people, experiences and challenges, we reexamine the way we think and feel about what Love means to us. The amazing thing is love is universal and touches us all in many ways. Love really is everywhere and I feel there are no wrong interpretations of the word Love.

I thought it would be a neat idea to gather quotes from all ages and incorporate them with pictures I have taken that resemble hearts. I've always loved taking pictures, capturing a moment in time and freezing it to share its beauty and truths with the world. I wouldn't call myself a photographer but I do absolutely adore taking them and what better way to share them with the world then to have them right alongside with people's thoughts on what love means to them.

I first got the idea for this book when I had realized I had taken well over a hundred pictures of things that resembled hearts. It had been about a three year period of time and I felt I needed to share them. This will be the first of 5 books and first up, children quote's. Needless to say, it was so fun to make this one. They had me laughing and smiling from ear to ear with all their silly, honest and off the wall thoughts about love. It was such an amazing experience that I'm glad to have had, and a special thank you to the children at Daniel Webster School in Pasadena, California. I couldn't have done this without all of you and their amazing Principal, Dr. Bauer. Thanks for your continuous support.

Each book will be geared at a different age range. Also, I'll be donating a percentage to specific foundations such as Saint Jude's hospital, children fighting cancer. Save the Arts which brings music programs back into schools, the Red Cross who families in need in times of crises and also Animal Rescue foundation that help animals find much needed loving homes and the LDF whom are dedicated to the long-term health and wellbeing of our planet as well as restoring balance to threatened ecosystems and communities. I hope you enjoy these books as much as I enjoyed making them... One of my favorite bands said it best, "All you need is love"

Agape,
Jessica ZavaLa

# *Introduction*

When I was a child I remember always being so painfully shy. I was the youngest of three and my mother was a single parent. She raised my brother, sister and I all on her own for a good amount of my childhood. She was a hard worker but also always in her own world, struggling with her own happiness as she made do with what little that she had to care for the three of us. I can only imagine the pain she must have felt with her overwhelming situation of raising us all on her own. Time consuming as it all was for her there was little time for love and affection, often times I hardly felt loved. I can't recall being told "I love you" more than a few times growing up. Not many kisses nor hugs. I feel because of it I always felt a sense of discontent as a child. Now that I'm a mother I notice I strive to make a comfortable, loving atmosphere for my daughter even though I too am a single parent. I always want her to feel loved and understood and not how I did growing up. The world around me seemed so complex and I didn't feel like I belonged much. I'd often observe people from a far. I never knew what to say when meeting new people. To those few who knew me well I was the chatty one with the long-winded stories, the jokester, trying to make those few in my small inner circle of people in my life, smile and feel happy but I always felt starved for attention and for recognition from my mother. I wanted to know I was doing a good job or was a good kid but never was able to find that comfort from her. I love and have a great amount of respect for her but even now unfortunately she and I don't have the relationship I would like us to have. I can remember like it was yesterday when I mentioned the idea of this book to her she replied "Oh, ok ummm. Well how many of these books do you actually think you're going to sell? You're actually going to publish this?" Instead of more of an encouraging response like "Congrats" "I'm so proud of you" "wow that's exciting" anything that would reflect some sort of encouragement. It goes without saying after hearing those words my heart broke a little more than it was before. I want to so badly see her in a positive light and in its own way she has taught me many lessons in unconditional love and tolerance. I also understand that we all love differently. We have our own style in which we project our love to others. I feel she raised me considering the circumstance the best she could. I don't want to hold resentment or anger, just acceptance after all she's the only mother I'll ever know.

This experience was one that touched my heart and brought me great joy. Most of the children in this book was selected by me from Daniel Webster School in Pasadena, California and I like to consider my little friends. I've been the classroom parent every year since my daughter was in kindergarten. She is now in 3rd grade and I've loved creating little bonds with many of the children here. I feel so blessed to be able to be involved with her and her class on every field trip, holiday activities, bringing the children treats and gifts during Christmas, Halloween, Valentine's Day and other holidays. Also volunteering in her class and at the school. It's been so amazing watching these children grow right before my eyes. It's a great feeling that's hard to describe in words what they make me feel when they see me at the school and they run to me while calling out my name "Ms. Jessica". Always greeting me with big smiles and little hugs, telling me stories about what happened during their day. Seeing their little faces light up makes my day that much better.

I wanted to create this book to allow others to share their own thoughts about what love means to them. It's something we all experience differently and interpret in our own way. The concept of what love is changes and evolves into a new way of thinking. This particular book was not originally planned out. All the pictures in this book have been taken by me over a 3 year period of time. It first started off with me taking pictures of things that resembled hearts. I remember finding them everywhere and in the most random places. I realized I had so many of them and thought I should put them all in a book. Then another idea came to mind. Quotes and not just any quotes but quotes from different people, in different stages of their life. I'm very fond of others point of views, even if it doesn't match up with mine. I think that is the beauty in life. We all have our own stories to tell and our own way of perceiving the world around us. So here it is. I hope you'll enjoy this series of books just as much as I enjoyed making them…

Love is the door which leads to the answers of life.
It takes great strength and faith to love and to be loved.
Love is like sun light to a flower, without it, it seizes to exist.

-Jessica Zavala

Love is when you care about your entire family.
Your brother, your sister, your uncle, your aunt, your
parents, grandma and grandpa too.

Ethan
Age 7

Love is complicated

Jolene
Age 9

Love is to have a crush on someone.

To like someone.

To marry someone.

Bella

Age 6

Love is when someone cares about you no matter what.

Rachel

Age 10

Love is helping your mom do stuff when she doesn't even ask you to.

Rodger
Age 8

Love is funny.

Mary

Age 7

Love means you share and care about everyone no matter what.

Joseph

Age 6

Love is when someone takes care of you.

Joshua

Age 7

Love is when my cousin taught me to snap my fingers. I didn't know how and she helped me to learn and now I know how. She didn't know how to whistle and I taught her how and now she knows how to whistle.

Jolene

Age 7

Love is when my mommy takes good care of me.

Kaden

Age 6

Love is crazy and silly...

Zoey

Age 5

Love is beautiful because love is like when you share your toys, your cookies and you can also share your Legos. I love my Legos!

Brooke
Age 6

Love is being happy and it means teaching people things. My cousin didn't know how to hula hoop so I taught him.

Daniela
Age 5

Love is ugly.

Marvin
Age 8

Love is when I help my little brother and sister.

Anthony

Age 8

Love is caring and sharing and love is really fun!

Zamairi

Age 5

Love is caring for other people.

Harlie

Age 8

Love is fun!

Tyler

Age 7

Love is silly and sometimes weird.

Rose

Age 7

Love is so beautiful cause you can share your last cookie
with your mom, your dad, your brother or sister.

Max

Age 8

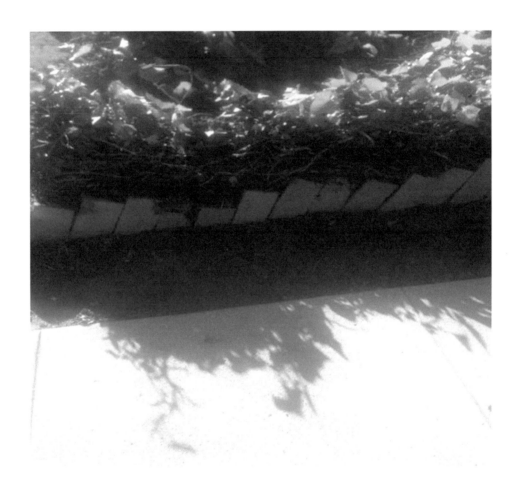

Love is when my dad broke his leg and I helped him get things around the house. He broke his leg and couldn't walk and had a cast on for a long time.

Victor

Age 8

Love is when I share with my baby brother and sister. And it's when you help people who don't have homes.

Alayna

Age 6

Love is when my mommy and daddy cook me and my brother breakfast. Pancakes, eggs and bacon. Oh and they're going to take me to Knotts Berry Farm for my birthday. It's coming up!

Denise
Age 7

Love is helping a friend when they get hurt.

Gopal

Age 8

Love is when you love your family. Love is when you share with your brothers and sisters and cousins. Love is when you pass by poor people and you might not have much money yourself but you still give them a little.

Jazmin

Age 8

Love is Beautiful...

Thomas
Age 7

Love is kind. It's a nice thing to say to people and share
with them too. It's being respectful too.

Gracie

Age 8

Love is caring for people, being nice to each other and also sharing your toys with your friends.

Olivia

Age 7

Love is serious.

Love is taking care of people and being kind.

Love is having friends.

Love is having lots of friends.

Robert

Age 8

Love is good. I love my mom and my mom takes good care of me.

James

Age 7

Love is swans, ducks and lopsided hearts…

Ela

Age 7

Love is when you watch out for your friends and your family.

Kristina

Age 10

Love is beautiful.

Arine
Age 10

Love is when you share and help and tell others what to do and they have to do it.

Olivia

Age 9

Love is ew!

August
Age 7

Love is when my mommy takes good care of me.

Anthony

Age 8

Love is being happy.

Knarik

Age 7

Love is caring and helping other people because its important.

Nareg

Age 8

Love means caring about someone even when you are mad
at them and want to hit them over their big head.

Jolie

Age 6

Love is pretty. Love is important. Love means
being kind. Its like a warm sunny day.

Jolene
Age 7

Love is feeling happy, peaceful and full of smiles.

Leslie

Age 8

Love is when I see my cat Brownie cuddling with her kittens. She is such a good mommy.

Rosie
Age 9

Love is feeling sad because your crush doesn't love you back.

Jason
Age 9

Love is when my mom wakes up to make my dad and me breakfast on a Sunday morning. Especially when she puts ice cream on my pancakes!!

Jacob

Age 8

Love is when my mom buys me the things I want even
when it is not my birthday or Christmas.

Carl
Age 8

Love is really weird and confusing sometimes.

Alex

Age 9

Love is when you tell someone they don't look fat wearing that when they ask you.

Wendy
Age 8

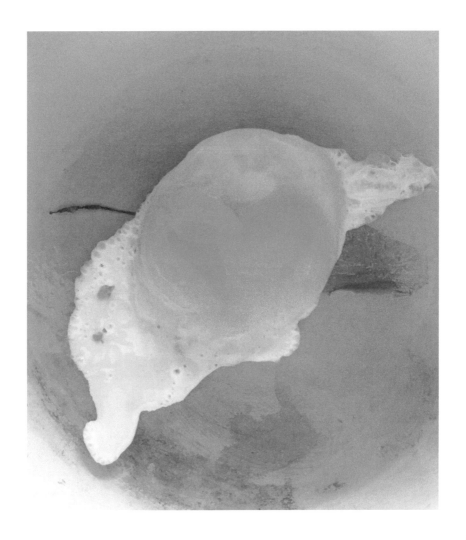

Love is went you make someone feel better because they are having a bad day. You help them see the good things in life and make them happy again. We all need to remember the good.

Cathy
Age 9

Love is when my dad text my mom out to a fancy
restaurant. He likes to surprise her.

Emily
Age 7

Love is when you stop other kids from bullying another kid at recess.
I hate to see kids being mean. The world needs more kindness.

Vanessa

Age 8

Love is when my dad brings my mom her favorite roses after they had a big fight so she can be nice to him again.

Brenda

Age 9

Love is when my dad takes out the trash when my mom didn't even have to ask.

Michael

Age 8

Love is when my dad helps my mom do the dishes after dinner.

Rebecca

Age 8

Love is a game for two and sometimes for three.

Mickey

Age 9

Love is when my family goes to the beach and we have lots
of fun playing in the water and making sandcastles.

Peter
Age 7

Love is ..... I don't know. I haven't met anyone that made me fall in love. But maybe when I'm in 3rd grade I will. I don't know.

Sean
Age 8

Love is when my mom lets me have cereal for dinner
instead the chicken and rice she made for us.

Kenny

Age 8

Love is always going to be there. It's stronger then anything. It will never go away because that person is so special. Even if they should die they will still be there to watch over you like your angel just there to protect you.

Audrey
Age 9

Love is beautiful and so lovely. I wish everyone could love each
other so the world could live in peace and harmony.

Max

Age 8

Love is like a mystery. No one can see it. It's just something you feel inside.

Serena

Age 7

Love is kind. It's being gentle and forgiving someone even when you don't want to.

Crystal
Age 8

Love is when my mom helps me with my homework
even when she is tired from working all day.

Jordan
Age 8

Love is crazy because it makes you feel like you are going to throw up when she walks into the classroom. She scares me.

Manual

Age 8

Love is sunshine, puppy dog tails and lolly pops.

Randy

Age 7

Love is really funny and makes you act very silly. I like it.

Matthew

Age 8

Love is so beautiful and great. I love my family a lot.

Melissa

Age 6

Love is when my dad lets my mom eat some of his ice cream
even when she said she didn't want a ice cream cone.

Christian
Age 10

Love is sharing cookies with your brother and sister even when you don't want to sometimes. Even when you want to eat them all.

Steven

Age 9

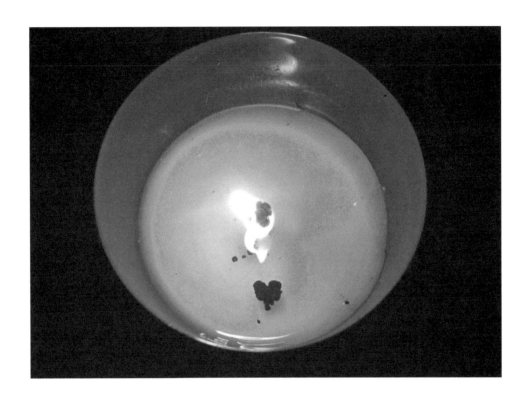

Love is sharing your toys and your games and your snacks.
It's being really nice to everyone you know.

Rebecca

Age 7

Love is when you help strangers that are poor or not happy. Love is very important because we all need it. We can all help each other if we try.

Jennifer

Age 10

Love is for everyone. It's for mommy and daddy. It's for
brothers and sisters. Love is for everyone.

Jake

Age 7

Love is when my mom buys me things and gets me
everything I want because I am a good boy.

Brandon
Age 6

Love is the best feeling because it makes you smile and makes you want to dance.

Thomas

Age 7

Love is when my brother helps me with my homework because he is older than me and I am still learning. He is almost 10 now. I don't like my homework.

Jacqueline

Age 7

Love is caring for each other.

Carter

Age 8

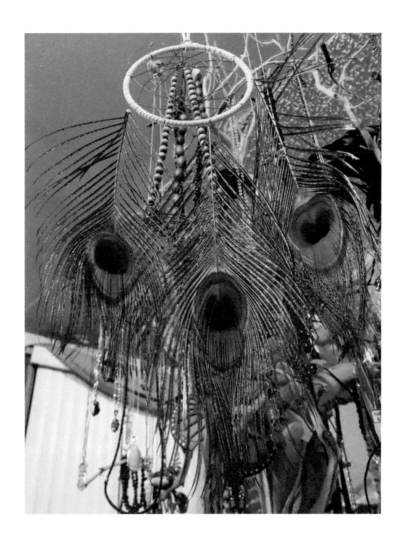

Love means to care for one another. It means we don't complain
and to love what we have. Love is a big heart filled with joy,
happiness and most importantly there is love.

Julia
Age 10

Love is kindness, like being nice to your family.

Lauren

Age 8

Love is life. You cannot live without love.

Logan

Age 9

*Follow me on Instagram at jzqueenofheartz*

For every book purchase a percentage will be donated to Adopt the Arts Foundation. This is an amazing program founded by one of my favorite bands, former drummer Matt Sorum from Guns N' Roses. It brings music programs back into schools. As a guitarist myself and a huge music junkie, I feel it's important for children to get the chance at experiencing the gift of learning and playing music. It can inspire a lifetime of creativity, hope, confidence and take you to a world of pure imagination...

Printed in the United States
By Bookmasters